OCEAN OF WISDOM

Guidelines for Living

The Dalai Lama
of Tibet

Winner of the Nobel Peace Prize

Foreword by Richard Gere
Photographs by Marcia Keegan

Clear Light Publishers
Santa Fe, New Mexico

This is a revised edition of
The Dalai Lama's Historic Visit to North America,
compiled and edited by Marcia Keegan. © 1981 Clear Light Publishers.

The eight Tibetan auspicious symbols and lotus on the jacket
were drawn by Phuntsok Dorje.

Editorial Consultants
J. Frances Tindall
Tinley Nyandak, Valerie M. Shepherd

Layout Design, Bud Wescott

Type Design, Bobbi Burger Brunoehler
Emery Printing, New York, N.Y.

Published by Clear Light Publishers,
823 Don Diego, Santa Fe, N.M. 87501

Published in Canada by McClelland and Stewart.

Library of Congress Card Catalog Number: 89-61093
ISBN: 0-940666-09-X
Printed in Hong Kong

The Nobel Peace Prize 1989

A Statement by the Norwegian Nobel Committee

The Norwegian Nobel Committee has decided to award the 1989 Nobel Peace Prize to the 14th Dalai Lama, Tenzin Gyatso, the religious and political leader of the Tibetan people.

The Committee wants to emphasize the fact that the Dalai Lama, in his struggle for the liberation of Tibet, consistently has opposed the use of violence. He has instead advocated peaceful solutions based upon tolerance and mutual respect in order to preserve the historical and cultural heritage of his people.

The Dalai Lama has developed his philosophy of peace from a great reverence for all things living and upon the concept of universal responsibility embracing all mankind as well as nature. In the opinion of the Committee, the Dalai Lama has come forward with constructive and forward-looking proposals for the solution of international conflicts, human rights issues, and global environmental problems.

Remarks by His Holiness the Fourteenth Dalai Lama of Tibet on being awarded the Nobel Peace Prize

I am deeply touched to be chosen as this year's recipient of the Nobel Peace Prize. I believe my selection reaffirms the universal values of non-violence, peace and understanding between all members of our great human family. We all desire a happier, more humane and harmonious world, and I have always felt that the practice of love and compassion, tolerance and respect for others is the most effective manner in which to bring this about.

I hope this prize will provide courage to the six million people of Tibet. For some forty years now Tibetans have been undergoing the most painful period in our long history. During this time, over a million of our people perished and more than six thousand monastaries — the seat of our peaceful culture — were destroyed. There is not a single family, either in Tibet or among the refugees abroad, which has gone unscathed. Yet, our people's determination and commitment to spiritual values and the practice of non-violence remain unshaken. This prize is a profound recognition of their faith and perseverance.

The demonstrations which have rocked Tibet for the past two years continue to be non-violent despite brutal suppression. Since the imposition of martial law in Lhasa last March, Tibet has been sealed off, and while global attention has focused on the tragic events in China, a systematic effort to crush the spirit and national identity of the Tibetan people is being pursued by the Government of the People's Republic.

Tibetans today are facing the real possibility of elimination as a people and a nation. The Government of the People's Republic of China is practicing a form of genocide by relocating millions of Chinese settlers into Tibet. I ask that this massive population transfer be stopped. Unless the cruel and inhuman treatment of my people is brought to an end, and until they are given their due right to self-determination, there will always be obstacles in finding a solution to the Tibetan issue.

I accept the Nobel Peace Prize in a spirit of optimism despite the many grave problems which humanity faces today. We all know the immensity of the challenges facing our generation; the problem of overpopulation, the threat to our environment and the dangers of military confrontation. As this dramatic century draws to a close, it is clear that the renewed yearning for freedom and democracy sweeping the globe provides an unprecedented opportunity for building a better world. Freedom is the real source of human happiness and creativity. Only when it is allowed to flourish, can a genuinely stable international climate exist.

The suppression of the rights and freedoms of any people by totalitarian governments is against human nature and the recent movements for democracy in various parts of the world is a clear indication of this.

The Chinese students have given me great hope for the future of China and Tibet. I feel that their movement follows the tradition of Mahatma Gandhi's ahisma or non-violence which has deeply inspired me ever since I was a small boy. The eventual success of all people seeking a more tolerant atmosphere, must derive from a commitment to counter hatred and violence with patience. We must seek change through dialogue and trust. It is my heartfelt prayer that Tibet's plight be resolved in such a manner and that once again my country, the Roof of the World, may serve as a sanctuary of peace and a resource of spiritual inspiration at the heart of Asia.

I hope and pray that the decision to give me the Nobel Peace Prize will encourage all those who pursue the path of peace to do so in a renewed spirit of optimism and strength.

October 5, 1989, Newport Beach, California

FOREWORD

by Richard Gere
Chairman of Tibet House, New York, N.Y.

This book contains the words of a great and completely worthy spiritual friend, the Fourteenth Dalai Lama, spiritual and temporal leader of the Tibetan people. From his mystical discovery as a small child in Amdo, to his ascension to the spiritual and temporal throne in Lhasa, to his thirty years in exile from the genocidal Chinese occupation of Tibet, his has been a life of action, responsibility, and sacrifice for the sake of all beings. It is his vast experience and very worldliness that lends such relevance to his universal teaching of kindness, compassion, and enlightened altruism.

My involvement with the Tibetans began in 1978 when I chanced upon a group of Tibetan refugees in the Nepalese Himalayas. Their suffering moved and shamed me greatly, yet I was touched by their resilience and lightness of spirit. In 1982 I met His Holiness the Dalai Lama. Years of Zen practice and study prepared me little for a physical encounter with such a man. I vaguely remember grinning and babbling like a fool. More clearly I recall the solidly expansive feeling of protection and wholeness that enveloped us. As open and profound as his own teachings, His Holiness is heart-breakingly present and real.

The message throughout this book is simple yet exceedingly difficult, a monumental teaching that is profoundly transforming and liberating. His words are seeds sown from his heart into ours. We need only open to receive them. May they bring happiness and the causes of future happiness.

INTRODUCTION

by Rinchen Dharlo
Representative of His Holiness the
Dalai Lama to North America

His Holiness the Fourteenth Dalai Lama, Tenzin Gyatso, was born on July 6, 1935 to a peasant family in the small village of Taktser in northeastern Tibet and was recognized at the age of two as the reincarnation of His predecessor, the Thirteenth Dalai Lama. The Dalai Lamas are the manifestations of the Buddha of Compassion, who chose to take rebirth to serve humanity. *Dalai Lama* means Ocean of Wisdom; Tibetans normally refer to His Holiness as *Yeshe Norbu*, the Wish-fulfilling Gem, or simply *Kundun*, the Presence. When the Thirteenth Dalai Lama died in 1935, the Tibetan Government had not simply to appoint a successor, but to discover the child in whom the Buddha of Compassion would incarnate; the child need not have been born just at the death of His predecessor, or even very soon thereafter. As before, there would be signs of where to search. For example, when the Thirteenth Dalai Lama's body was laid in a shrine facing south, His head turned to the east twice, and to the east of this shrine a great fungus appeared on the east side of a pillar of well-seasoned wood. The Regent of Tibet went to the sacred lake of Lhamoe Lhatso, where Tibetans have seen visions of the future. There he saw, among other things, a monastery with roofs of jade green and gold and a house with turquoise tiles. A detailed description of the entire vision was written down and kept a strict secret.

In 1937 high lamas and dignitaries were sent throughout Tibet to search for the place seen in the vision. Those heading east were led by Lama Kewtsang Rinpoche of Sera Monastery. In Taktser they found such a place and went to the house, with Kewtsang Rinpoche disguised as a servant and a junior monk posing as the leader. The Rinpoche was wearing a rosary of the Thirteenth Dalai Lama, and the little boy, recognizing it, demanded that it be given to him. This was promised, if the child could guess who the wearer was. The reply was *Sera aga* (in the local dialect, a monk of Sera). The boy was also able to tell who the real leader and servant were. After many further tests, the new Dalai Lama was enthroned in 1940.

In 1950, at the age of sixteen and still facing nine more years of intensive religious education, His Holiness had to assume full political power when China invaded Tibet. In March of 1959, during the national uprising of the Tibetan people against Chinese military occupation, He went into exile. Since then He has lived in the Himalayan foothills in Dharamsala, India, the seat of the Tibetan Government-in-exile, a constitutional democracy since 1963. Dharamsala, aptly known as Little Lhasa, also has cultural and educational institutions and serves as a "capital-in-exile" for 130,000 Tibetan refugees living mainly in India; others are in Nepal, Switzerland, the UK, the United States, Canada, and thirty other countries. In the past decade, the Dalai Lama has tried to open a dialogue with the Chinese. He proposed a Five-Point Peace Plan in 1987-88, which would also stabilize the entire Asian region and which has drawn widespread praise from statesmen and legislative bodies around the world, but the Chinese have yet to enter into negotiations.

Meanwhile, the Fourteenth Dalai Lama, unlike His predecessors who never came to the West, continues His worldwide travels, eloquently speaking in favor of ecumenical understanding, kindness and compassion, respect for the environment, and, above all, world peace.

My message is the practice of compassion, love, and kindness.

These things are very useful in our daily life, and also for the whole of human society. Their practice can be very important.

Wherever I go, I always give the advice to be altruistic and kind to others. And from my own point of view, I am concentrating my own energies, meditation, and so forth, on the increase of kindness. This is essential, essential Buddhadharma.

❂

Great compassion is the root of all forms of worship.

❂

Whether one believes in a religion or not, and whether one believes in rebirth or not, there isn't anyone who doesn't appreciate compassion, mercy.

❂

Right from the moment of our birth, we are under the care and kindness of our parents. And then later on in our life, when we are oppressed by sickness and become old, we are again dependent, on the kindness of others. And since at the beginning and end of our lives, we are so dependent on others' kindness, how can it be in the middle that we neglect kindness towards others?

If one assumes a humble attitude, one's own good qualities will increase. Whereas if one is proud, one will become jealous of others, one will become angry with others, and one will look down on others. Due to that, there will be unhappiness in society.

One of the basic points is kindness. With kindness, with love and compassion, with this feeling that is the essence of brotherhood, sisterhood, one will have inner peace. This compassionate feeling is the basis of inner peace.

With anger, hatred, it is very difficult to feel inner peace. It is on this point that various different religious faiths all have the same emphasis. In every major world religion, the emphasis is on brotherhood.

Those who are kind and useful to us are like our parents. We can extend this love by regarding ourselves as a member of the human family in an interdependent world, relying on others for our welfare and comfort. Also, if we have a kind and loving heart we will win more friends. We will feel better. Such a motivation may be selfish. But, if we are selfish with wisdom, then we will realize the need to love others, near and far, even our enemies. This is one way of generating love.

The Potala Palace in Lhasa, Tibet. The former
residence of the Dalai Lamas.

His Holiness the Dalai Lama on the set of CBC's
"Man Alive" program in Toronto, Canada.

It is the enemy who can truly teach us to practice the virtues of compassion and tolerance.

Wars arise from a failure to understand one another's humanness. Instead of summit meetings, why not have families meet for a picnic and get to know each other while the children play together?

In olden times when there was a war, it was a human-to-human confrontation. The victor in battle would directly see the blood and suffering of the defeated enemy. Nowadays, it is much more terrifying because a man in an office can push a button and kill millions of people and never see the human tragedy he has created. The mechanization of war, the mechanization of human conflict, poses an increasing threat to peace.

We know that in the event of a nuclear war there will be no victors because there will be no survivors. Is it not frightening to contemplate such inhuman and heartless destruction? And is it not logical that we should remove the cause of our own destruction when we know it and when we have both the time and means to do so? Often, the reason we cannot overcome a problem is that we are ignorant of its cause or powerless to remove this cause. Such is not the case with the nuclear threat.

By far the greatest single danger facing humankind — in fact, all living beings on our planet — is the threat of nuclear destruction. I need not elaborate on this danger, but I would like to appeal to all the leaders of the nuclear powers who literally hold the future of the world in their hands, to the scientists and technicians who continue to create these awesome weapons of destruction, and to all the people at large who are in a position to influence their leaders: I appeal to them to exercise their sanity and begin to work at dismantling and destroying all nuclear weapons.

The governments of the United States and Russia meet and talk in political symbols. They spend time studying political nuances, the meaning behind the meaning. Why not talk directly in straightforward terms?

I have always believed that human determination and truth will ultimately prevail over violence and oppression. Today important changes are taking place everwhere in the world which could profoundly affect our future and the future of all humanity and the planet we share. Courageous moves by world leaders have facilitated the peaceful resolution of conflicts. Hopes for peace, for the environment, and for a more humane approach to world problems seem greater than ever before.

The Christians and Buddhists have basically the same teaching, the same aim. The world now becomes smaller and smaller and smaller, due to good communications and other factors also. With that development, different faiths and different cultures also come closer and closer. This is, I think, very good. If we understand each other's way of living, thinking, different philosophies, and different faiths, it can contribute to mutual understanding. By understanding each other, naturally we will develop respect for each other. From that, we will develop true harmony and the ability to make joint efforts. And I always feel that this special inner development is something very important for mankind.

No one knows what will happen in a few decades or a few centuries, what adverse effect, for example, deforestation might have on the weather, the soil, the rain.

We are having problems because people are concentrating on their selfish interests, on making money, and are not thinking of the community as a whole. They are not thinking of the earth and the long-term effects on man as a whole. If we of the present generation do not think about them now, the future generation might not be able to cope with them.

The Dalai Lama and Paul Cardinal Gregoire, Archbishop of Montreal.

Under the bright sun, many of us are gathered together with different languages, different styles of dress, perhaps even different faiths. However, all of us are the same in being humans, and we all uniquely have the thought of "I," and we're all the same in wanting happiness and in wanting to avoid suffering.

But at the root, there are two kinds of pleasure and suffering. There are physical and mental pleasures and physical and mental sufferings. Our materialistic progress is for the sake of achieving that happiness which depends on the body and for getting rid of that suffering which depends on the body. However, it is indeed difficult, isn't it, for us to get rid of all suffering by external means? And thus there comes to be a great difference between seeking happiness by dependence on material things and in seeking happiness by dependence on one's own internal thought. Although the basic suffering is the same, there comes to be a great difference in the way we experience this, depending on our attitude. Therefore, mental attitude is very important with respect to how we spend our lives.

A good mind, a good heart, warm feelings — these are the most important things. If you don't have such a good mind, you yourself cannot function. You cannot be happy, and so also your own kin, your own mate or children or neighbors and so forth won't be happy either.

And thus from nation to nation and continent to continent, everyone's mind becomes disturbed, people lose happiness. But then, on the other hand, if you have a good attitude, a good mind, a good heart, then the opposite is true.

Thus in human society, love, compassion, and kindness are the most important. They are really precious; they are very necessary in your own life. So it is worthwhile to make an effort to develop this sort of good, good heart.

Calm abiding of the mind, meditative stabilization, and wisdom are the weapons. Wisdom is like the bullet or the ammunition, and the calm mind is like the weapon for firing.

Just as when we fight external suffering, we have to undergo suffering, and so forth, so when we undergo any strife internally, there is indeed internal pain. Therefore, religion is something internal to be thought about.

There is no need to mention the great difference between the amount of satisfaction there is in just oneself being happy and the amount of satisfaction there is in an infinite number of people being happy.

If even one person cannot stand suffering, what need is there to mention how all people can't stand suffering? Therefore, it is a mistake if one uses others for one's own purpose; rather one should use oneself for others' welfare. Thus one should use whatever capacities of body, speech, and mind one has for the benefit of others: That is right. Thus it is necessary to generate an altruistic mind and wish that the welfare of others is increased through their achievement of happiness and through their getting rid of suffering.

It is in dependence upon sentient beings that one first generates this altruistic aspiration to highest enlightenment, and it is in relation to sentient beings that one practices the deeds of the path in order to achieve enlightenment, and it is for the sake of sentient beings that one achieves Buddhahood. Therefore, sentient beings are the object of observation, the basis of all of this marvellous development. Therefore, they are more important than even the wish-granting jewel, and one should treat them respectfully and kindly.

With the basic understanding of all humans as brothers and sisters, we can appreciate the usefulness of different systems and ideologies that can accommodate different individuals and groups which have different dispositions, different tastes. For certain people under certain conditions, a certain ideology or cultural heritage is more useful. Each person has the right to choose whatever is most suitable. This is the individual's business on the basis of deep understanding of all other persons as brothers and sisters.

Deep down we must have real affection for each other, a clear realization or recognition of our shared human status. At the same time, we must openly accept all ideologies and systems as means of solving humanity's problems. One country, one nation, one ideology, one system is not sufficient. It is helpful to have a variety of different approaches on the basis of a deep feeling of the basic sameness of humanity. We can then make a joint effort to solve the problems of the whole of humankind. The problems human society is facing in terms of economic development, the crisis of energy, the tension between the poor and rich nations, and many geopolitical problems can be solved if we understand each others' fundamental humanity, respect each others' rights, share each others' problems and sufferings, and then make a joint effort.

Even if we cannot solve certain problems, we should not regret it. We humans must face death, old age, and disease as well as natural disasters, such as hurricanes, that are beyond our control. We must face them; we cannot avoid them. But these sufferings are quite sufficient for us — why should we create other problems due to our own ideology, just differing ways of thinking? Useless! It is sad. Thousands upon thousands of people suffer from this. Such a situation is truly silly since we can avoid it by adopting a different attitude, appreciating the basic humanity which ideologies are supposed to serve.

❁

According to Buddhist psychology, most of our troubles are due to our passionate desire for and attachment to things that we misapprehend as enduring entities. The pursuit of the objects of our desire and attachment involves the use of aggression and competitiveness as supposedly efficacious instruments. These mental processes easily translate into actions, breeding belligerence as an obvious effect. Such processes have been going on in the human mind since time immemorial, but their execution has become more effective under modern conditions. What can we do to control and regulate these "poisons" — delusion, greed, and aggression? For it is these poisons that are behind almost every trouble in the world.

14

One's own anger, pride, and so forth serve as obstacles to the development of one's own altruistic attitude. They harm it. They injure it. Therefore, one shouldn't just let these go on when they are generated, but, by relying on antidotes, stop them.

Anger, pride, competitiveness, and so forth are our real enemies. So, since there isn't anybody who hasn't gotten angry at some time, we can, on the basis of our own experience, understand that no one can be happy with an attitude of anger.

What doctor is there who prescribes anger as a treatment for any disease? What doctor is there who says that by getting angry one can make oneself happier?

Anger, hatred, jealousy — it is not possible to find peace with them. Through compassion, through love, we can solve many problems, we can have true happiness, real disarmament.

One of the most important things is compassion. We cannot buy it in one of New York City's big shops. We cannot produce it by machine. But by inner development, yes. Without inner peace, it is impossible to have world peace.

Now I am going to say something about how to develop this compassion.

First of all, it is important to understand that between you and others, others are far more important, because others are far more numerous.

If you don't use your imagination just to make up something, sometimes imagination can be used very effectively in order to understand a point. Therefore, in your mind please imagine that on one side is one party made up of all beings, an infinite number of beings. And on the other side, imagine another party, that is to say, your single, selfish self.

Now you're thinking as a third person. Now, if you think properly, would you go to this side, with this single, selfish man, or to this side, with the limitless other? Naturally, you will feel much closer to the limitless other, because of the number of beings.

But both are the same human beings. Both have a desire for happiness. The only difference is number. So, if limitless number is much more important, then naturally you will join this party.

In this way, you can see that others are far more important than you and that all of your capacity could be used for the benefit of others.

Love is an active human condition. When certain problems arise, you will feel hate, you may feel anger. In order to practice tolerance, first you have to control anger. Some people might think that it is better to express your anger than to control it. But among our conceptions, there are two types, one of which it is better to control. One class of conceptions consists of thoughts which lead to depression and so forth. With those, it is definitely helpful if you are able to express those thoughts. However, there is a whole different class of conceptions, such as hatred and love, which, when they are expressed once, aren't used up, they just increase. We can, in our own experience, understand that when desire and hatred and so forth are generated, we can watch them and figure out techniques by which we can lessen them. Through my own little experience, I can show you. If we can control some of our anger, which we can change ourselves, and if, on the other hand, we can think of the importance of other people's welfare and practice in this way, then it is possible to achieve these good attitudes.

You see, practice of this is ultimately of benefit to you. If you are truly selfish, wisely selfish, this practice gives you real calmness, and with inner calmness and peace you can handle all these problems with ease.

❁

In our human life, tolerance is very important. If you have tolerance, you can easily overcome difficulties. If you have little tolerance or are without it, then the smallest thing immediately irritates you. In a difficulty, you may overreact. In my own experience, I've had many questions, many feelings, and one of these feelings is that tolerance is something to practice worldwide in our human society.

So who teaches you tolerance? Maybe sometimes your children teach you patience, but always your enemy will teach you tolerance. So your enemy is really your teacher. If you have respect for your enemy instead of anger, your compassion will develop. That type of compassion is real compassion, which is based upon sound beliefs.

Usually you allow kindness toward family members. This kindness is inspired by affection, desire. Because of that, when the object of your compassion changes in aspect, becomes a little rough, then your own feeling changes also. That kind of compassion or love is not right. Therefore, it is necessary in the beginning to train these good attitudes.

From all points of view, we're all the same in wanting happiness and not wanting suffering. Now you are only one, but others are infinite in number. Therefore, others are more important than you.

When it is said that one should be patient and withstand trouble, that doesn't mean that one should be defeated, should be overcome. The very purpose of engaging in the practice of patience is to become stronger in mind, stronger in heart. And also you want to remain calm. In that atmosphere of calm, you can use real human beings to learn wisdom. If you lose patience, if your brain founders by emotions, then you've lost the power to analyze. But if you are patient, from a basis of altruism, then you don't lose your strength of mind; you can even increase your strength of mind and then use your powers of analysis to figure out ways to overcome the negative force that is opposing you. That's another question.

Material facilities, material encounters are very necessary for a human society, a country, a nation. They are absolutely necessary. At the same time, material progress and prosperity in themselves cannot produce inner peace; inner peace should come from within. Thus, much depends upon our own attitude toward life, toward others, particularly toward problems. When two persons are facing the same kind of problem, because of different mental attitudes it is much easier for one person to face the problem. So you see, it's the internal viewpoint that makes the difference.

If we put to use our more subtle consciousnesses, there will be that many more things that we can use the mind for. Therefore, qualities that begin in the mind can be increased limitlessly.

❂

When one gives one's kindness for the sake of getting something back in return, for the sake of getting a good name, for the sake of causing other people to like oneself, if the motive is for self, then this would not be really a Bodhisattva deed. Therefore, one-pointedness points to giving only for the sake of helping others.

❂

Compassion and love are precious things in life. They are not complicated. They are simple, but difficult to practice.

Compassion can be put into practice if one recognizes the fact that every human being is a member of humanity and the human family regardless of differences in religion, culture, color, and creed. Deep down, there is no difference.

Since everybody belongs to this world, we must try to adopt a good attitude worldwide, a good feeling for our fellow brothers and sisters. In my particular case, we Tibetans are carrying on a struggle for our rights. Some say that the Tibetan situation is only political, but I feel it is not. We Tibetans have a unique and distinct cultural heritage just as the Chinese have. We do not hate the Chinese; we deeply respect the richness of Chinese culture which spans so many centuries. Though we have deep respect and are not anti-Chinese, we six million Tibetans have an equal right to maintain our own distinctive culture as long as we do not harm others. Materially we are backward, but in spiritual matters — in terms of the development of the mind — we are quite rich. We Tibetans are Buddhists, and the Buddhism which we practice is a rather complete form of Buddhism. Also, we have kept it active, very much alive.

In the past century we remained a peaceful nation with our unique culture. Now, unfortunately, during the last few decades, this nation and culture are being deliberately destroyed. We like our own culture, our own land; we have the right to preserve it.

I am serving our cause with the motivation of service to humankind, not for reasons of power, not out of hatred. Not just as a Tibetan but as a human being, I think it is worthwhile to preserve that culture, that nation, to contribute to world society. This is why I am persisting in our movement, and though some people see this as a purely political matter, I know it is not.

We hope very much that the overall attitude of the People's Republic of China is changing, but we are cautious due to our past experience. I do not say this out of a wish to criticize; rather, it is a fact. Upon investigation you can determine whether it is fact or not; time will tell.

We human beings have a developed brain and limitless potential. Since even wild animals can gradually be trained with patience, the human mind also can gradually be trained, step by step. If you test these practices with patience, you can come to know this through your own experience. If someone who easily gets angry tries to control his or her anger, in time it can be controlled. The same is true for a very selfish person; first that person must realize the faults of a selfish motivation and the benefit in being less selfish. Having realized this, one trains in it, trying to control the bad side and develop the good. As time goes by, such practice can be very effective. This is the only alternative.

Without love, human society is in a very difficult state; without love, in the future we will face tremendous problems. Love is the center of human life.

I maintain that every major religion of the world — Buddhism, Christianity, Confucianism, Hinduism, Islam, Jainism, Judaism, Sikhism, Taoism, Zoroastrianism — has similar ideals of love, the same goal of benefiting humanity through spiritual practice, and the same effect of making their followers into better human beings. All religions teach moral precepts for perfecting the functions of mind, body, and speech. All teach us not to lie or steal or take others' lives, and so on. The common goal of all moral precepts laid down by the great teachers of humanity is unselfishness. The great teachers wanted to lead their followers away from the paths of negative deeds caused by ignorance and to introduce them to paths of goodness.

❂

We are going into deep outer space based on developments of modern technology. However, there are many things left to be examined and thought about with respect to the nature of the mind, what the substantial core of the mind is, what the corroborative condition of the mind is, and so forth. There is much advice, many precepts with respect to this, but the meaning of all of these is love and compassion. Within the Buddhist doctrine, there are very many powerful techniques capable of advancing the mind with respect to compassion and love.

It is said that someone who acts as an enemy toward you is your best teacher. Now, by depending on teachers, you can learn about the importance of being patient but you can't get any opportunity actually to be patient. However, the actual practice of implementing patience comes when meeting with an enemy.

If we understand the oneness of humankind, then we realize the differences are secondary. With an attitude of respect and concern for other people, we can experience an atmosphere of happiness. That way we can create real harmony, real brotherhood. Through your own experience, try to be patient. You can change your attitude. If you practice continuously, you can change. The human mind has such potential — learn to train it.

If you have love and compassion toward all sentient beings, particularly toward your enemy, that is true love and compassion. Now the kind of love or compassion that you have toward your friends, your wife, and your children is essentially not true kindness. That is attachment. That kind of love cannot be infinite.

I believe that because of Tibetan art and culture, many foreign visitors come to Tibetan settlements in India and Nepal to meet Tibetans. At the beginning, we ourselves did not notice certain things, certain thinking, but these foreigners, after visiting, said, "Why you Tibetans have some sort of honest, happy life — very good despite your suffering. What is your secret?"

There is no secret. But I thought to myself, our culture is very much based on compassion. We are used to saying all the time, always, "All sentient beings are our fathers and mothers." Even someone who looks like a ruffian or a robber is still someone who has on his mind, "All mothers, all sentient beings." So I myself always practice this thinking. I think that is the real cause of happiness.

✵

With regard to the Bodhisattva vehicle, there is no practice that is not included within the basic motivation of consciously seeking the highest enlightenment of the Buddha for the sake of all living beings, this being induced by love and compassion and attained through the practice of the Six Perfections.

Some of you might feel that you lose your independence if you don't let your mind just wander where it wants to, if you try to control it. But that is not the case.

If your mind is proceeding in the correct way, you already have the correct opinion. But if your mind is proceeding in an incorrect way, then it's necessary, definitely, to exercise control.

If you ask, "Is it possible to completely get rid of afflicted emotions or is it necessary to just suppress them on the spot," then the answer, from the Buddhist point of view, is that the conventional nature of mind is a clear light. And from the ultimate point of view, it is also a clear light. So from the conventional point of view, these afflicted emotions are only extraneous and can be removed totally.

❁

Inner darkness, which we call ignorance, is the root of suffering. The more inner light that comes, the more darkness will diminish. This is the only way to achieve salvation or *nirvana*.

Today, human society's major problem is human rights. Through highly developed scientific technology, we can solve any material human problem, such as poverty, disease, etc., but at the same time, due to this same technology, we create more fear and more desire. For example, today we fear a sudden explosion of atoms in the world. That sort of thing has become a reality.

Now you see, if we have such fears — of potential destruction from the atom bomb — we will suffer greatly from them unless we have inner peace. On top of the usual human suffering, we have more fear, more constant threat. So therefore we need more the teachings of kindness and feelings of brotherhood.

In order to live together on this planet, we need kindness, we need a kind atmosphere rather than an angry atmosphere. To solve problems, we need a warm atmosphere.

So although there are various social/religious factors that may differ, all religions have this goal of creating inner peace.

We need to clearly recognize that the basic aim of all religions is the same. Since all religions are for the sake of taming our minds to make us better persons, we need to bring all religious practice into a healing of our minds. It's not at all good, and extremely unfortunate, to use the doctrines and practices that are for the sake of taming the mind as reasons for becoming biased. Therefore it is extremely important for us to be nonsectarian. As Buddhists, we need to respect the Christians, the Jews, the Hindus, and so on. Also, among Buddhists we shouldn't make distinctions and say that some are Theravadin and some are of the Great Vehicle and so forth; we are all the same in having the same teacher. If we become more sundered under this influence of bias due to obscuration, then there is no end to it. Therefore, we need to recognize that the religious doctrines are for the sake of taming the mind and use them that way.

❂

The principles that are set forth in the Theravada scriptures revolve around wisdom, selflessness, and the practice of meditation, which includes the development of the thirty-seven harmonies with enlightenment. These truths have as their basis the good effort of not harming others. Therefore, their basis is compassion.

In order to increase the sense of cherishing others, it is first important to think about the faults of cherishing ourselves and the good qualities of cherishing others. If we cherish others, then both others and ourselves, both deeply and superficially, will be happy. Whether in terms of the family or of the family of nations as a whole world, if we take the cherishing of others as the very basis of policy for our format, then we will be able to succeed in our common effort. Most of the good or beneficial effects that come about in the world are based on an attitude of cherishing others.

The opposite is also true. When we cherish ourselves more than others, both superficially and deeply, we produce various types of suffering, both for ourselves and for those around us. Therefore, we need to make an effort at the root of this goodness, that is to say, this good heart, warm heart.

Now we have to consider — if we want to increase the basic good attitude — that the type of closeness that we have for the class of our own friends is very small and it cannot be extended forever. What we have to do, however, is to change it and increase it and extend it. Now we, our friends and all living beings, are alike in wanting happiness and in not wanting suffering. We are equal in this way. And both you and others have the right to get rid of suffering and to gain happiness. On the basis of these equalities, you are only one, whereas others are infinite in number.

The many scriptures set forth in the teachings of Buddha are included in three scriptural collections. How is it that all of the Buddha's teachings are included in three scriptural collections? It is that the Buddha set forth the three trainings. The three trainings are included in the three scriptural collections, because each of them serves as the means of expressing mainly one of those collections, one of those trainings. What are the three trainings? There is the training in ethics. This training as set forth includes the mode of behavior. Then there is the training in meditative stabilization, which explains how to meditate. The Dharma is indeed practiced by way of body, speech, and mind, but mainly by way of mind. One needs to tame the mind. One needs a strong mind, a concentrated mind. Therefore, one needs to develop calm abiding. In the effort to attain wisdom, what we don't want is suffering, and in order to get rid of suffering, we need the intelligence that can discriminate between the good and bad, and so forth. Therefore, we need wisdom.

The scriptures that take these three as the main objects of teaching are, respectively, the scriptural collection of discipline, the scriptural collection of the set of discourses, and the scriptural collection of knowledge. The training in ethics is concerned with behavior; the training in meditative stabilization is concerned with meditation; the training in wisdom is concerned with view. There is the triad: view, behavior, and meditation. The scriptures set forth a mode by which one's view, behavior, and meditation will not fall in either of the two extremes.

The scriptures on discipline set forth modes of behavior for a lay person and for monks and nuns. In the discipline, it sets forth a prohibition against the extreme of having excessively good clothing, food, shelter, and so forth. And the Buddha also prohibited the extreme of self-torture, in which one engages in too much fasting or wears clothing that is not appropriate such that it brings suffering to oneself. Therefore, our proper behavior is achieved in the proper context of not falling into either of these two extremes. As Shantideva said in his *Engaging in Bodhisattva Deeds*, "The main thing is to consider the situation; what is needed in the situation."

When one puts these precepts into practice, one needs to consider that which is to be done and the purpose. For instance, for a monk or a nun, it is not permitted to eat after 2:00 p.m. However, there are exceptions; for instance, if a person has an illness such that if that person didn't eat it would increase the illness. Similarly, one is also not allowed to lie. For instance, suppose someone has a vow to tell the truth and is in the woods and sees an animal run off in a certain direction. Then the hunter comes along and asks the person where the animal went. There is a prohibition against lying, but the purpose here would be for the sake of saving the life of that animal. Therefore, at that time, the person who has taken the vow not to lie can say, "Oh, I really didn't see anything," or "I saw something in the trees." As illustrated by this, one has to take into account that which is prohibited and the probable benefit of doing something some other way, and one has to do that which is more beneficial.

With respect to meditation, if, for instance, one's mind comes under the influence of factors that are not consistent with meditative stabilization, such as excitement or laxity, then that is one extreme. The purpose of overcoming the distractions of laxity or excitement is to make one's mind so that one is capable of meditating on the actual mode of existence of phenomena, and thus be able to cultivate a true view. But if one, having gotten rid of laxity and excitement, only cultivates a nonconceptual state, then that is an extreme, and that nonconceptual state will only lead to another lifetime of rebirth in cyclical existence, in a higher type of realm.

So, roughly speaking, that is a way of avoiding the two extremes — through the effects of meditation.

Then when one explains the view, this is done in terms of the two truths. Sometimes this is expressed as appearance and emptiness. All systems, whether Buddhist or non-Buddhist, present their view in terms of avoiding the two extremes of permanence and nihilism: the Santyas, the Vedantas, or, within Buddhism, the Vaibhasikas, the Sautrantikas, the Chittamatrins, and the Madhyamikas.

For instance, within the Buddhist systems themselves, from within their own specific viewpoint, each of them, to their own mind, has set forth a view that avoids the two extremes. However, when their views are analyzed with subtle reasoning, then the higher schools find the lower schools to have fallen into extremes of permanence or nihilism. So, then, how is it that the higher schools can refute the lower, given that both are based on Buddhist teachings?

In the Buddhist system, the Buddha set forth the four reliances: Do not rely on the person; rely on the doctrine. You cannot say that a doctrine is to be valued just because a person who teaches it is something wonderful. Rather, it is the case that whether the person is reliable or not is to be proved by the reliability or lack of reliability of the doctrine that the person teaches.

Then, with respect to the doctrine, one shouldn't rely on the euphony and so forth of the words but look to the profundity of those words. Then, with respect to the teachings, one should not rely on the meaning to be interpreted but on the definitive meaning. And with respect to the meaning, one should not rely on the consciousness that is deluded or affected by dualistic perception, but rather one should rely on an exalted wisdom consciousness that is free from such dualistic appearances.

Therefore, the teacher, Buddha himself, said, "Oh monks and nuns, you should not accept my teaching just out of respect for me but should analyze it the way that a goldsmith analyzes gold by rubbing, cutting, and melting." Therefore, although Buddha himself set forth several means of distinguishing his own scriptures with respect to whether they were definitive or interpretable, it is by reasoning that we must determine which are definitive and which are interpretable.

Thus it is that the entire system, with subtler and subtler

reasoning, shows that two of the lower systems fall into the two extremes. How is it, in the Madhyamika system, that they avoid the two extremes? They avoid the extreme of permanence by holding the view that phenomena do not exist in their own right. And it is through knowledge of how to present all the actions, objects of cyclic existence, and *nirvana* — how to present all phenomena within the context of their not existing inherently but conventionally, validly — that they avoid the extreme of nonexistence or nihilism.

It is truly the mind that sees the actual mode of subsistence of phenomena. It is the mind that acts as an antidote to the types of aimless consciousness that misconceive the nature of phenomena. And it is through removing that ignorance that one can remove the desire and hatred and so forth that are induced by that ignorance. When one can stop that, one can stop the accumulation of contaminated actions, or *karma*. Through stopping that, one stops birth. Through stopping birth, one stops suffering. Such a training in wisdom can only be achieved by the mind; therefore, it is necessary to make the mind serviceable. Therefore, I see it as necessary prior to the training in wisdom to engage in the training of meditative stabilization.

I feel that the essence of all spiritual life is your emotion, your attitude toward others. Once you have pure and sincere motivation, all the rest follows. You can develop this right attitude toward others on the basis of kindness, love, and respect, and on the clear realization of the oneness of all human beings. This is important because others benefit by this motivation as much as anything we do. Then, with a pure heart, you can carry on any work —farming, mechanical engineering, working as a doctor, as a lawyer, as a teacher — and your profession becomes a real instrument to help the human community.

❁

I believe in justice and in human determination. In the history of man it has already been proved that the human will is more powerful than the gun. And also in the Tibetan case, the Tibetan nation has more than 2,000 years experience in dealing with China, with India and Nepal, with Outer Mongolia and other human communities.

So although for us this is the toughest period, I quite firmly believe that the Tibetan people, their culture, and the Tibetan faith will survive, will once again flourish. This I always believe.

Buddhists believe in beginningless rebirth. So certain bad *karmas* which may not have been created in a certain lifetime may have been created in some other lifetime. It is also not necessary to have accumulated the bad *karmas* at one time and at one place. Different beings at different times and places may have accumulated the same amount of *karma*. They then get born at one time and at one place. The suffering that they undergo is the result of their common karmic effect.

Today, we are having this beautiful weather; we are enjoying this together at one place and at the same time. But the *karma* which gave us this opportunity may have been accumulated by us at different places. Yet the result is that we are all experiencing this together at this moment and at this place. It is not necessary that on account of our having the same experience now we should have created the cause of this particular moment at one place jointly.

You have to practice kindness and follow the teachings. At the same time, if you always practice tolerance, compassion, sometimes some people may take advantage of you. On such occasions, without losing your internal calmness, your internal compassion, you may take an action of some nature in order to prevent someone from taking advantage of you. That is a practical way. You have to avoid the extreme, too, of being taken advantage of. At all times, one needs to avoid the two extremes. If you get too hungry, the same — if you gorge yourself, the same also.

Within each nation, the individual's inalienable right to happiness ought to be recognized and, among different nations, there must be equal concern for the welfare of even the smallest nation. I am not suggesting that one system is better than another and that all should adopt it. On the contrary, a variety of political systems and ideologies is desirable to enrich the human community, so long as all people are free to evolve their own political and socioeconomic system, based on self-determination. If people in poor countries are denied the happiness they desire and deserve, they will naturally be dissatisfied and pose problems for the rich. If unwanted social, political, and cultural forms continue to be imposed by one nation upon another, the attainment of world peace is doubtful.

The most difficult problems in the world, which, in large part, emanate from the most developed societies, stem from an overemphasis on the rewards of material progress, one that has placed in jeopardy the very aspects of our common heritage that, in the past, inspired human beings to be honest, altruistic, and spiritually mature. It is clear to me that material development alone cannot replace the old spiritual or humanitarian values that have been responsible for the progress of world civilization as we know it today. We should try, I feel, to strike a balance between material and spiritual growth. I have heard a great many complaints about material progress from Westerners, yet, paradoxically, this progress has been the pride of the Western world. I see nothing wrong with material progress per se, provided man is given precedence over his creations. Although materialistic knowledge has contributed enormously to human welfare, it is not capable of creating lasting happiness. In the United States, where technological development is perhaps more advanced than in any other country, there is still a great deal of mental suffering. This is because materialistic knowledge can only provide the type of happiness that is dependent upon physical conditions; it does not provide the happiness that springs from inner development independent of external factors.

There should be a balance between material and spiritual progress, a balance achieved through the principles based on love and compassion. Love and compassion are the essence of all religion.

All religions can learn from each other; the ultimate goal of all religion is to produce better human beings. Better human beings would be more tolerant, more compassionate, and less selfish.

If all your energy and all your thinking are concentrated on wealth, on material things (all that wealth belongs to *this* life), there is a maximum benefit for one hundred years. Beyond that there's nothing.

"Empty" means selfless, noninherent existence, absence of any inherent existence. It is like zero; if you look, zero itself is zero, nothing. But it is something; without a zero we cannot make 10 or 100. Similarly, the emptiness: it is emptiness; at the same time it is the basis of *everything*. In other words, we cannot find any *thing*. We will just find emptiness. As to their nature, things do not exist in accordance with how they appear. Since there is something, an object, therefore we can investigate, for it means there is something. But its own nature is empty of inherent existence; emptiness is the nature of the object. So because of emptiness, it appears and disappears. The living being is born and disappears; suffering comes and goes; happiness comes and goes. All these things, all these changes, appearing and disappearing, can be possible *because* of emptiness, because of the nature of the non-self-existence. If suffering, suffering as well as bliss, were independent, then it could not change. If it would not depend on causes or factors, then it would not change. Because there is this reality of emptiness, it is possible for the changes and transformation of the objects that are empty to take place. And the very change and transformation of the objects themselves are an indication or a sign, a sign of the reality of emptiness.

❂

It is not being said that in order to generate a consciousness which has arisen through hearing or from thinking that realizes emptiness, it is necessary at first to engage in the training of meditative stabilization. What is being said is that in order to generate a consciousness which has arisen from meditation and realizes emptiness, it is necessary at first to engage in the training of meditative stabilization.

In order to overcome the internal distractions within the mind, it is necessary at first to overcome the distractions of body and speech through proper ethics. Therefore, the training in ethics is set forth first. But the series of degrees are set forth in their series of practices. That is the explanation of how to avoid the two extremes in relation to the three trainings.

You new Buddhists in Western society need also to avoid the two extremes. One of these extremes would be complete isolation from the general way of life and also from society. That is the same thing. It is better to remain in society and to lead a general way of life. That's my belief.

And the other extreme would be to become completely absorbed in this worldly life, to become so involved in making money that one becomes a part in a machine. So you have to avoid those two extremes.

So my true religion is kindness. If you practice kindness as you live, no matter if you are learned or not learned, whether you believe in the next life or not, whether you believe in God or Buddha or some other religion, in day-to-day life you have to be a kind person. With this motivation, it doesn't matter whether you are a practitioner or a lawyer or politician, administrator, worker, or engineer. Whatever your profession or field, you carry your work as a professional. In the meantime, deep down, you are a kind person. This is something useful in daily life.

From my viewpoint all things first originate in the mind. Things and events depend heavily on motivation. A real sense of appreciation of humanity, compassion, and love are the key points. If we develop a good heart, then whether the field is science, agriculture, or politics, since motivation is so very important, these will all improve. A good heart is both important and effective in daily life. If in a small family, even without children, the members have a warm heart to each other, a peaceful atmosphere will be created. However, if one of the persons feels angry, immediately the atmosphere in the house becomes tense. Despite good food or a nice television set, you will lose peace and calm. Thus, things depend more on the mind than on matter.

The Himalayan mountains.

Man in Lhasa, Tibet raises a picture of the Dalai Lama to his head as a form of blessing to himself. The most precious gift for a Tibetan is to receive a picture of the Dalai Lama.

We might ask: how do the different levels of the consciousness or mind that apprehends an object actually come to exist themselves? Different levels of consciousness established are in relation to the different levels of subtlety of the inner energy that activates and moves the consciousness towards a given object. So, the level of their subtlety and strength in moving the consciousness towards the object determines and establishes the different levels of consciousness. It is very important to reflect upon the relationship between the inner consciousness and outer material substances. Many Eastern philosophies, and in particular Buddhism, speak of four elements: earth, water, fire, and air, or five elements with the addition of space. The first four elements, earth, water, fire, and air, are supported by the element of space, which enables them to exit and to function. Space or "ether" serves, then, as the basis for the functioning of all the other elements.

These five elements can be divided into two types: the outer five elements and the inner five elements, and there is a definite relationship between the outer and inner elements. As regards the element space or "ether," according to certain Buddhist texts, such as the Kalachakra Tantra, space is not just a total voidness, devoid of anything at all, but it is referred to in terms of "empty particles." This empty particle therefore serves as the basis for the evolution and dissolution of the four other elements. They are generated from it and finally are absorbed back into it. The process of dissolution evolves in the order: earth, water, fire, and air, and the process of generation in the order: air, fire, water, and earth. These four are better understood in terms of: solidity (earth), liquids (water), heat (fire) and energy (air). The four elements are generated from the subtle level to the gross, out of this basis of empty particles, and they dissolve from the gross level to the subtle into the empty particles. Space, or the empty particle, is the basis for the whole process.

The "Big-Bang" model of the beginning of the universe has perhaps something in common with this empty particle. Also, the most subtle, fine particle described in modern physics seems to be similar to the empty particle. Such parallels do present something that I feel it would be worthwhile to reflect upon.

✦

His Eminence Ganden Tri Rinpoche, the head of the Tibetan Buddhist Gelugpa School, performing a ceremony at an altar at the Newark museum.

Tibetan monk in India.

From the spiritual point of view of Buddhism, the state of our mind, whether it is disciplined or undisciplined, produces what is known as *karma*. This is accepted in many Eastern philosophies. *Karma*, meaning action, has a particular influence upon the inner elements which in turn affect the outer elements. This, too, is a point for further investigation.

Another area in Tibetan Buddhism which may be of interest to scientists is the relationship between the physical elements and the nerves and consciousness, in particular the relationship between the elements in the brain and consciousness. Involved here are the changes in consciousness, happy or unhappy states of mind, etc., the kind of effect they have on the elements within the brain, and the consequent effect that has on the body. Certain physical illnesses improve or worsen according to the state of mind. Regarding this kind of relationship between body and mind, Buddhism can definitely make a contribution to modern science.

Buddhism also explains, with great precision, the different levels of subtlety within consciousness itself. These are very clearly described in the Tantras, and research on these, in my opinion, would produce very beneficial results. Consciousness is classified, from the point of view of its level of subtlety, into three levels: the waking state or gross level of consciousness, the consciousness of the dream state which is more subtle, and the consciousness during deep, dreamless sleep, which is subtler still.

Similarly, the three stages of birth, death, and the intermediate state are also established in terms of the subtlety of their levels of consciousness. During the process of dying, a person experiences the innermost, subtle consciousness; the consciousness becomes grosser after death in the intermediate state, and progressively more gross during the process of birth. Upon the basis of continuity of the stream of consciousness is established the existence of rebirth and re-incarnation. There are currently a number of well-documented cases of individuals who clearly remember their past lives, and it would seem that it would be very worthwhile to investigate these phenomena, with a view to expanding human knowledge.

Human beings are of such nature that they should have not only material facilities but spiritual sustenance as well. Without spiritual sustenance, it is difficult to get and maintain peace of mind.

To maintain wisdom, it is necessary to have inner strength. Without inner development, sometimes we may not retain self-confidence and courage. If we lose these things, life will be difficult. The impossible can be possible with willpower.

49

His Holiness talking to a child at a gathering of schoolchildren.

Richard Gere with His Holiness's sister-in-law, Kunyang Norbu (left), and His Holiness's sister, Jetsun Pema (right), standing in front of the Tibetan stupa consecrated by His Holiness the Dalai Lama in 1987 in Bloomington, Indiana. This stupa, built by Professor Thubten Jigme Norbu, older brother of the Dalai Lama, is in memory of 1.2 million Tibetans who lost their lives for Tibet's freedom.

To increase your compassion, visualize yourself, first, as a neutral person. Then on the right side, visualize your old self as a person who is only seeking his or her own welfare, who doesn't think at all about other people, who would take advantage of anyone whenever the chance arises, and who is never content. Visualize your old self that way on the right.

Then on the other side of your neutral self, visualize a group of persons who are really suffering and need some help. Now think: All humans have the natural desire to be happy and to avoid suffering; all humans equally have the right to be happy and get rid of suffering. Now you think — wisely, not selfishly — and even if some selfishness must be there, think in a widely selfish way, not in a narrow-minded, selfish way: Everybody wants happiness; nobody wants foolishness or wants that type of selfish, discontented person.

So you see, if you want to be a good person, a more reasonable, logical person, then you don't want to be like this narrow-minded, selfish person on the right. You don't want to join this single, selfish, greedy, discontented person on the right. It's almost like making a line between the single selfish person and the group: You want to join that group.

When you practice this technique of visualization, naturally the majority side wins your heart. As you come closer to the majority side, by that much you get farther away from this selfishness. Because the mediator of this is yourself, your own sense of altruism will increase and increase. If you practice this way daily, it will be helpful.

❁

If we use this human brain for something of little import, that is very sad. If we spend our time just concerned with the affairs of this lifetime up to the point of death, that is very sad and weak. We need to decide that it is completely perverse. When we think in this manner, the emphasis just on this lifetime becomes weaker and weaker. It is said that we should renounce this life. That doesn't mean that we should go hungry or not take care of this lifetime at all but that we should reduce our attachment to affairs that are limited to this lifetime. Now, when we reduce the emphasis on the appearances of this lifetime and the appearances of future lifetimes come to the mind, it is necessary to investigate those also. Because in the future, even though one attains a good lifetime, there will be a lifetime after that lifetime, and a lifetime after that lifetime.

❁

The Dalai Lama addressing an interfaith service at
the Wilshire Boulevard Temple in Los Angeles.

His Holiness receiving Hopi Elders (left to right)
Earl Pela, Thomas Banyacya, and David Monongye,
in Los Angeles, California in 1979.

If you tame your mind, happiness comes. If you don't tame your mind, there is no way to be happy. It is necessary to fix up the mind. It is through the appearance of these afflicted emotions in your mind that you are drawn into various bad actions and so forth. But if these afflicted emotions which appear in the expanse of the nature of the mind can be extinguished back into the nature of the mind, then the afflicted emotions and actions and so forth that are built on them will stop. As Milarepa said, "Like clouds appearing from space and disappearing back into space."

If your mind is dominated by anger, you will lose the best part of the human brain: wisdom, the ability to decide between what is right and what is wrong. Anger is the most serious problem facing the world today.

All major religions are basically the same in that they emphasize peace of mind and kindness; but it is very important to practice this in our daily lives, not just in a church or a temple.

There is no sense in just being attached to this lifetime, because no matter how long you live in this type of life nowadays, at the longest around 100 years, at that time you must die. At most then. Otherwise, it's not definite when you will die. But no matter how much wealth and resources you have in this lifetime, it won't help at all at that point.

If you become very rich, even become a millionaire or a billionaire, on the day of your death, no matter how much money you have in the bank, there isn't any little piece of it that you can take with you. The death of a rich person and the death of a wild animal, each is just the same.

❋

The mind of enlightenment is the wish for clear enlightenment, complete and perfect enlightenment, for the sake of others. In cultivating in detail this altruistic mind of enlightenment, which has the two intentions of helping others and achieving one's own enlightenment in order to do that, there are two streams of transmission of instruction. The one is from Asanga, the *Sevenfold Cause and Effect Instructions*, and the other is the *Switching of Self and Other*, transmitted through Nagarjuna to Shantideva, Shantideva being the one who explained it in great detail.

Shantideva's *Engaging in Bodhisattva Deeds* is really excellent for this. Nagarjuna also sets forth a brief and fundamental way in his *Precious Garland*. Use *Precious Garland* as the root text, and use Shantideva as the explanation of it. For those who want to generate this altruistic mind of enlightenment, these two are really necessary.

One should cultivate, in meditation, an attitude of equanimity, and then meditate on all sentient beings as being mothers, fathers, brothers, and sisters. Once one generates this attitude of equanimity for the three beings, having gotten over desire and hatred, one needs to remove the factor of neglect that can be present when people are viewed equally. This can be done in two different ways: one is through generating a sense of altruism, wishing to help those beings because they want happiness and don't want suffering, and the other is to reflect upon the kindness of those beings toward oneself. It is through reflecting on how sentient beings have helped oneself, have been one's father and mother and so forth, over the continuum of lifetimes and through realizing that it would be unsuitable to deny them proper help that one can train the attitude of wishing for help and happiness for sentient beings.

When one gets used to these types of thoughts, the mind can be gradually trained. Someone who is extremely selfish but who begins to cultivate such habits will gradually become less and less selfish. So then this is how one generates the sense of altruism toward others.

If in all situations, no matter what the mind is doing, from a corner of the mind one is still intensely seeking the welfare of sentient beings and seeking enlightenment for the sake of them, then one has generated a fully qualified altruistic mind of enlightenment. These types of real-izations are not such that when you generate them, the whole world turns around for them. One's disposition changes gradually, gradually.

If you cultivate this slowly, steadily, over a period of time, then when five, ten years have passed, when you consider your way of life, your way of thinking and so forth, how it was before and how it is now, then you can see the difference.

❈

Liberation cannot be sought from the outside through something else — like someone else giving it to you. When one has achieved liberation by means of removing all afflicted emotions, then no matter what kind of external conditions one meets with, one will not generate any of the afflicted emotions. Thus one will not newly accumulate any new *karma*. The cycle has been stopped.

Therefore, the attainment or the nonattainment of liberation depends on the removal or the nonremoval of the afflicted emotions, the chief of which is ignorance. The process of liberation depends on the removal of the afflicted emotions, and that depends on wisdom. Wisdom in turn depends on the intention to definitely get out of cyclic existence. Initially it is very important to develop the intention to leave cyclic existence.

In the sphere of international relations … a sense of greater or shared responsibility is particularly needed. Today, when the world is becoming increasingly interdependent, the dangers of irresponsible behavior have dramatically increased. In ancient times, problems were mostly family-size and were solved at the family level. Unless we realize that now we are part of one big, human family, we cannot hope to bring about peace and happiness. One nation's problems can no longer be solved by itself because so much depends on the cooperation of other states. Therefore, it is not only morally wrong, but pragmatically unwise, for either individuals or nations to pursue their own happiness oblivious to the aspirations of others who surround them. The wise course should clearly be based on seeking a compromise out of mutual self-interest.

❂

If you get to the point where a corner of your mind is continuously involved with the wish to achieve highest enlightenment for the sake of sentient beings, then that's the time when this altruistic mind of enlightenment needs to be conjoined with the actual rite of mind generation — the wishing rite of generating the mind of enlightenment.

And having done that, one needs to train in the causes that prevent that aspiration of mind from deteriorating in this lifetime or in later lifetimes. It is not sufficient just to generate this aspiration. One needs to generate the actual mind of enlightenment, the actual intention to become enlightened for the sake of others. The intention alone is not sufficient. One needs to train in order to understand that it is necessary to engage in the practices to bring about full enlightenment, these being the practices of the six perfections (giving, ethics, patience, effort, concentration, and wisdom) or the ten perfections.

Now having trained in the wish to generate the actual mind of enlightenment, it is necessary to undertake the Bodhisattva vows. If, having taken the Bodhisattva vows, one's practice of the Bodhisattva deeds is going well, then it is possible to enter into the practice of Tantra or Mantra.

The reason the Buddha made this display of leaving all the facilities of a household and becoming a monk, going into retreat, meditating, and so forth, was in order to indicate to us, his followers, what we should do. If the Buddha had to work very hard to achieve realization, it's pretty much impossible that we could achieve the same realization by taking it easy.

❂

It is one thing to explain the Dharma from the mouth, but it is very hard to put it into practice. If you don't put the Dharma into practice, however, there is no way for a good fruit to become ripe, just by explaining. If the cause is just something explained from the mouth, the effect would be just something explained from the mouth, and that wouldn't help much, would it? When we are hungry, what we need is some actual food. It's not going to help for someone to say, "Oh, French food is very tasty, English food is very tasty," and so forth. In time you will get fed up with the person just saying these things to you and will be in danger of getting angry. When I indicate the path of liberation to you, you need to put it into practice. Shantideva says, "As it is with medicine, it's not sufficient just to touch it, it is necessary to take the medicine internally."

In order to generate the thought to get out of cyclic existence, it is necessary to know about the good qualities of liberation and the faults of cyclic existence that one wants to get out of. However, what is cyclic existence? As Dharmakirti says, it can be posited as the burden of mental and physical aggregates which are assumed out of contaminated action. Therefore, cyclic existence doesn't refer to some sort of country or area. When you look into it, cyclical existence can be identified as the burden of these mental and physical aggregates which we have assumed from our own contaminated actions and afflicted emotions.

When once we have such contaminated aggregates, they serve as a basis of suffering in the present. Because they are under the influence of former contaminated actions and afflicted emotions, they are not under their own power.

That they are not under their own power means that, even though we want happiness and don't want suffering, we are beset by many sufferings. This is because we have this type of mind and body which is under the influence of former contaminated actions and afflictions. And these contaminated mental and physical aggregates also induce suffering in the future.

Every religion of the world has similar ideals of love, the same goal of benefiting humanity through spiritual practice, and the same effect of making their followers into better human beings. The common goal of all moral precepts laid down by the great teachers of humanity is unselfishness. All religions agree upon the necessity to control the undisciplined mind that harbors selfishness and other roots of trouble. And each, in its own way, teaches a path leading to a spiritual state that is peaceful, disciplined, ethical, and wise, thus helping living beings to avoid misery and gain happiness. It is for these reasons that I have always believed all religions, essentially, have the same message. Therefore, there is a great need to promote better interfaith understanding, leading to the development of reciprocal respect for one another's faith. I also believe, for obvious reasons, that religion itself has much to offer in the achievement of peace.

❂

We talk about peace a great deal. But peace has a chance to exist only when the atmosphere is congenial. We must create that atmosphere. In order to do that we must adopt the right attitude. Peace therefore must basically first come from within ourselves. And why should we strive for peace? For the simple reason that peace is of benefit to us in the long run and that we therefore desire it.

The questions and answers that follow were compiled from the Dalai Lama's numerous public and private lectures, scholarly seminars, private meetings, and news conferences.

❁   ❁   ❁

Q: How do you feel Tibetan Buddhism is being practiced in America?

A: The important thing is to get the essence. In Tibetan Buddhism there are a great variety of practices and many different methods of practicing. All are beneficial. At the same time, while taking the essence, there might be certain traditional ways of practicing which might have to undergo change in order to adjust to the new environment or social structure. In the past, when a religion has gone from its native country to a new land, the essence was brought. Then, within that new land, it developed and adjusted to new circumstances. Something similar should happen to Tibetan Buddhism. So, it is your responsibility.. I don't know.

Q: Do you think the West can learn from Tibetans?

A: I think so.

Q: You were trained as a monk from childhood. Should American children be trained in a system from an early age, or should we wait until later?

A: There are two ways to enter into Buddhism: one through faith and one through reasoning. At present — in this century, on this earth, in this period — for a Buddhist faith alone may not be sufficient. So, reasoning is very important. Because of this, it would be better for someone to be trained later. But, nevertheless, it would make a difference if a child knew the influence within the family from a very young age.

Q: Western upbringing focuses on the individual first. We focus on getting there very quickly, going very high. Can you offer us a simple lesson about social responsibility?

A: I think that you need to explain the basic structure of human community, of the human species ... You need to teach the idea that as a human being you need some kind of sense of responsibility for others. Can this be introduced to children? Teach them to show kindness to insects. It's time for elder people to listen to the child's voice. You see, in the child's mind there is no demarcation of different nations; no demarcation of a different social system or ideology. Children know, in their mind, that all children are the same, all human beings are the same. So, from that viewpoint, their minds are more unbiased. Then when people get older they start to say, "Our nation, our religion, our system." When an "us" and "them" demarcation develops, then people don't bother about what happens to others, except to "us" or "me." It's easier to introduce social responsibility to a child than to an adult. It is a noble idea. It's very important to introduce these right ideas, not as a religious matter, but simply as a matter of one's own further happiness, one's own future success. You can take an example from the history books: those people who use too much cruelty, too much selfishness, and are self-centered, may gain fame and certain things on a temporary basis. But nobody has much respect for people like Hitler or Stalin. At one time they may become very powerful, but that comes from cruelty or aggression. That fame is not the right fame, and nobody shows deep respect for that. In other cases the fame of people like Abraham Lincoln or Mahatma Gandhi comes from a different side, a different aspect. People respect their work.

So you see, introduce children to the importance, the value, and the benefit in positive thought, in kindness, and in forgiveness.

Parental affection, close physical contact, loving kindness for all living beings, social responsibility and special attention to the less privileged — these are all concepts we know. They are not difficult to understand, but their practice is often forgotten. In this time of emphasis on home life, family, personal well-being, and help for the homeless, these ideas are ones which we all could demonstrate. For the sake of our children, let's remember to teach them kindness.

Q: Do you think that the Tibetan Buddhism practiced in America is authentic?

A: It depends to a great extent on the people who are teaching it, those who are doing the teaching.

Q: Are there some who are more authentic than others?

A: I will answer by giving some explanation about Buddhism. In general, in Buddhism it is said, rely not on the person, rely on the doctrine. Similarly, whether the person is valid and reliable or not depends upon what the person is saying. One should not rely just on the fame of the person. Therefore, someone who is going to practice Buddhism must analyze well. If, having analyzed, he finds that it is beneficial and dependable, then it's suitable to engage in that practice. It is said that even if it takes twelve years to engage in such analysis, it's suitable. That's our general attitude. I can't say anything about particular people. In general, many people are serving the Buddhist teaching, and that's good. At the same time, it is important to be cautious. In the past, in our own country, and also in China, Mongolia, and Russia, Buddhist monasteries were originally learning centers. This was very good. In some cases, due to social influence, these centers became corrupt. Sometimes they became more like centers for business and money-making than religious centers. So in the future we must take care. Also, we welcome constructive criticism from our friends. This is very important. Not to just believe too much praising — criticism is very necessary.

Q: *There's a strong feeling in the West that for something to be good, it must have some concept of permanence. The religions that had their origin in India do not have this, and I think this is the basic problem that the West has in understanding these other ways of thinking.*

A: The purpose of religion is not arguing. If we look for them, we can find many differences. There is no use talking about it. Buddha, Jesus Christ, and all other great teachers created their own ideas, teachings, with sincere motivation, love, kindness toward humankind, and they shared it for the benefit of humankind. I do not think these great teachers made these differences in order to make more trouble.

I make distinctions in order to get peace in your own mind, not for criticizing, not for argument or competition. Buddhists can't make the whole world population become Buddhist. That's impossible. Christians cannot convert all mankind to Christianity. And Hindus cannot govern all mankind. Over the past many centuries, if you look unbiasedly, each faith, each great teaching, has served mankind very much. So it's much better to make friends and understand each other and make an effort to serve humankind rather than criticize or argue. This is my belief.

Also, if I say that all religions and philosophies are the same, that is hypocritical, not true. There are differences. I believe there's a 100% possibility to make real peace and to help shoulder to shoulder and serve humankind. Equally, we have no responsibility and no right to impose on a nonbeliever. What's important is that a nonbeliever or a believer is likewise a human being; we must have a lot of respect for each other.

Q: Is it possible to have world harmony?

A: Whether we can achieve world harmony or not, we have no other alternative but to work toward that goal. It is the best alternative we have.

Q: With the vision of world unity, in your tradition is there any prediction of any such event coming about and is there any record of it existing in the ancient past?

A: No.

Q: Individuals almost never say they favor warfare, but they make war. Why?

A: Basically, it is ignorance. There are many different states of mind. Reasoning is needed when the mind is emotional and thoughts of anger, hatred, and attachment are strong. Then it is hopeless to reason. When these feelings are the general atmosphere, then almost always there is tragedy.

Q: *Do you think that some day you will return to a free Tibet?*

A: Certainly.

Q: *How?*

A: That's for time to tell. I can only say that things do change, and already there are communications.

Q: *What would you like Americans to do about the Chinese presence in Tibet?*

A: We are fighting for our own happiness, our own rights. After all, we Tibetans are human beings. We have the right to live as a human brotherhood, we have the right to gain our happiness. In this country, people always regard the importance of freedom, the importance of liberty, which we also want.

Q: *How do you suggest that we, as spiritual people, can effect a spiritual influence, practically speaking, on political affairs?*

A: This is a difficult question. The atmosphere is not healthy. Everyone says peace, but when things are related to self-interest, nobody bothers about war, killing, stealing, etc. That's the reality. Under such circumstances, you have to be temperate and practical. We need some long-range policy. I feel deeply that maybe we can find some new type of educational system for the younger generation, with an emphasis on love, peace, brotherhood, etc. One or two countries cannot do this; it must be a worldwide movement. So, practically, we who believe in moral thinking must live our way of life as something truthful, something reasonable, and make it like an example, a demonstration to others, of the value of religion, the value of spirituality. That we can practice, that is our responsibility. Before teaching others, before changing others, we ourselves must change. We must be honest, sincere, kindhearted. This is very important. This doesn't just apply to your question. This is the responsibility of all mankind.

Q: Where does Buddhism stand on social reform?

A: One of the basic Buddhist philosophies is the theory of interdependence. Many types of good and bad and benefit and harm are determined in Buddhism with respect to the actual situation at the particular time. Therefore, it's difficult with respect to many topics to say that only one particular way is the correct one. Thus, there have to be many changes.

Q: Who is the individual responsible to, or what are the motives for his moral responsibility?

A: The reason why we seek to behave in a good manner is that it's from good behavior that good fruits are derived. So, the basic reason is that one wants happiness and doesn't want suffering, and on the basis of that, one enters into good actions and avoids bad actions. Goodness and badness of actions are determined on the basis of the goodness and badness of their fruits. Thus, this involves the Buddhist doctrine of *karma* and the effects of action. Similarly in Hinduism, too.

Q: *Is the intention of an action important?*

A: Yes, certainly. Motivation. This is the most important, the keypoint. We make differences between *karma*, for instance, when one doesn't have the motivation but has done the deed, or has the motivation but hasn't done the deed, or both, or neither.

Q: *There is a breakdown in institutions — in religion and in family. How do you feel that we can reverse that trend?*

A: Through moral ethics, consideration and patience and more and more tolerance of each other, and, of course, compassion. First of all, before people get married, they should decide and be careful and not go into it in a rushed manner out of infatuation. And gradually undertake the right feeling for family life and atmosphere. I feel it is extremely important. When I have seen a child whose parents are divorced, I felt very sorry, because I think for the rest of his or her life somehow it affects the child.

Q: *What responsibility do Buddhists have in dealing with people who cause suffering?*

A Buddhist monk doing a ritual dance.

His Holiness at the Green Gulch Buddhist Center in California.

A: You have to make an attempt to stop it.

Q: *Is the difference between the empirical self and the actual self what is common to all religions?*

A: There are differences within the Buddhist schools on this. There are different positions presented with respect to what "I" is. Eight different interpretations! Everyone accepts that there is the mere "I" and that this appears to those whose minds have and have not been affected by systems, and if one denies that there is such an "I" or self, this would contradict direct perception. Because Buddhism asserts selflessness, when one doesn't understand what the word "self" is or what selflessness means, there's a danger of thinking that there's no "I" or self at all. If one doesn't accept an "I" or self in any way whatsoever, then this would be a falling into an extreme of nihilism.

Q: *You appear to be a very hopeful man. In the past, we've had such great tragedies as the holocaust, tragedies of totalitarian nations, tragedies in this country against Native Americans, yet you're hopeful. What is the basis of your hope?*

A: Hope is the basis of hope. I mean, there is no guarantee, but it's better to hope and try. Actually, our basic human way of life is on the basis of hope. The long-term hope is that truth will overcome. Historically, we've had all those bad fights, but fighting never remains forever; sooner or later that will cease, that will diminish.

Q: Your Holiness, has your exile from Tibet brought about changes in Tibetan philosophy?

A: Philosophy? I don't think so. The Buddhist philosophy is based on reason. Philosophy is the main point of my country. The essence of Dharma will not change. As long as reality remains the same, philosophy will be the same. As long as humans face suffering, there will remain the Dharma, which deals not only with human beings but with all sentient beings in this condition.

Q: From a national level, does altruism run the risk of sacrifice? How do you practice altruism for a neighbor who seeks to destroy you?

A: That is a complicated question. From this viewpoint, our second generation, the refugees, are more the problem. You see, it would be better to forget than to continue to hold anger, but it is very complicated, because in the future we don't know where we will be. So there is no other alternative but to think we have to do something for the growth of kindness. We have to think and work to make a new world.

Actually, in our life there is no telling if we will live tomorrow, but we are doing our usual business in the hope that we will survive tomorrow. Though there is no telling what the future will hold, one must do something or try to do something. This is the right thing.

The completed Kalachakra mandala.

The Namgyal monks carefully place grains of
colored sand on a Tibetan Kalachakra mandala.
The Kalachakra is a traditional Buddist ritual
ceremony dedicated to peace and physical balance
both for individuals and for the world.
The Kalachakra mandala is created for use in this
ceremony, after which the sands are swept away.

Q: Your Holiness, can you explain how your successor might be chosen due to the changes in the situation in Tibet as to the way in which you were chosen, as you explained. And can you explain how any changes might be made in the way of succession?

A: I have not much worry about it. If the Tibetan people feel it necessary to choose another Dalai Lama, all right, then they will choose a Dalai Lama. If people feel it not necessary, not much better to do so, then no Dalai Lama will exist. But that's not my responsibility. I hope I'll remain for some time. But choosing another Dalai Lama is the next generation's responsibility.

Q: You had spoken about the notions of kindness and selfishness and suffering and happiness mainly from the point of view of the single person. But how do groups such as nations achieve kindness, unselfishness, and happiness? What is the step from the individual to the group? How can one make a group altruistic?

A: Groups are composed of individual persons. Our atmosphere and environment nowadays are very strained, not very peaceful ones. In our atmosphere today, things are decided by money and power. This is not right. The present atmosphere is due to our own mode of thinking. Now in order to change it, first we have to, as individuals, take the initiative in trying to develop certain good human qualities. First of all, we need to make a demonstration of what a good attitude and a good mode of behavior is, person by person by single person, then gradually over time build groups that have this attitude. Now, with this education, how do we utilize this education? If a person really has altruism, then to the extent that that person gains knowledge of various sufferings, that person can put it to use to help others.

Q: *Your Holiness, would you give us a brief outline of how you came to your spiritual mission in your life?*

A: It seems I feel my mission is, wherever I am, to express my feeling about the importance of kindness and the true sense of brotherhood. This I always feel, and I myself practice this. For the Tibetan community I express these things, and I advise them on the importance of kindness and on the need to develop less attachment, more tolerance, more contentment. These are very useful and very important. Generally, wherever I go, in the United States, in Europe, in Mongolia, I stress the importance of kindness, and it seems to me that generally people agree with my feelings. So I feel that they hold my vision also.

Anyway, from my side, I am trying to uplift real human brotherhood. I think human harmony is based on a true sense of brotherhood. As a Buddhist, it doesn't matter whether we are believers or nonbelievers, educated or uneducated, Easterners or Westerners or Northerners or Southerners, so long as we are the same human beings

His Holiness giving the Kalachakra initiation in Madison, Wisconsin, in 1981. It is said the Buddha first offered the teachings and blessings for this initiation in South India 2,500 years ago.

A Namgyal monk preparing for an initiation in front of the Kalachakra thanka (a religious painting on fabric).

with the same kind of flesh and the same kind of features. Everyone wants happiness and doesn't want sorrow, and we have every right to be happy.

Sometimes we humans put too much importance on secondary matters, such as differences of political systems or economic systems or race. There seem to be many discriminations due to these differences. But comparatively basic human well-being is not based on these things. So I always try to understand the real human values. All these different philosophies or religious systems are supposed to serve human happiness. But there is something wrong when there is too much emphasis on these secondary matters, these differences in systems which are supposed to serve human happiness. When human values are lost for these things, it is not much good.

So, in a few words, it seems my mission is the propagation of true kindness, genuine kindness and compassion. I myself practice these things. And it gives me more happiness, more success. If I practice anger or jealousy or bitterness, then I am sure I will give the wrong impression. More sadness. No doubt my smile would disappear if I practiced more anger. If I practice more sincerity or kindness, it gives me more pleasure.

Q: Do you believe that there is a view of religion that will unify mankind internationally?

A: I think it's helpful to have many different religions, since our human mind always likes different approaches for different dispositions. Just like food. There are some people who prefer bread and some who prefer rice and some who prefer flour. Each has different tastes, and each eats food that accords with his own taste. Some eat rice, some eat flour, but there is no quarrel. Nobody says, "Oh, you are eating rice." In the same way, there is mental variety. So for certain people the Christian religion is more useful, more applicable. It's a basic belief. Some people say, "There's a God, there's a Creator, and everything depends on His acts, so you should be impressed because of the Creator." You see, if that sort of thing gives you more security, more belief, you will prefer that approach. For such people, that philosophy is the best. Also, certain people say that our Buddhist belief that there is no creator and that everything depends on you, you should be impressed — that that is preferable. You see, if you are master, then everything depends on you. For certain people, that way of seeing is much more preferable, much more suitable.

So from that point of view, it is better to have variety, to have many religions.

✡

Now if these words are helpful for you, then put them into practice. But if they aren't helpful, then there's no need for them.